Kristine Hope

The Storm:

Anthology 2012-2021

Unless otherwise indicated, all the names, characters, businesses, places, events and incidents in this book are either the product of the author's imagination or used in a fictitious manner. Any resemblance to actual persons, living or dead, or actual events is purely coincidental.

Copyright © 2023 Kristine Hope

All rights reserved. No part of this book may be reproduced or used in any manner except for use of brief quotations in a book review.

First paperback edition June 2023

Book design by HopePoetry

Library of Congress Control Number: 2023910109

ISBN (paperback): 979-8-218-21815-7

Published in the USA by HopePoetry LLC

www.hopepoetry.com

Introduction

Poetry is an expression of a poet's soul. These poems may contradict, reiterate topics, go on tangents, and delve into the darkness of the mind. They are fragments of myself and my most prized possessions.

This anthology includes a selection of poems written over a decade from the age of thirteen to twenty-three. I continue to write and will do so until the day that I die. It is my lifeline.

Contents

The Storm 2012 1
    The Storm 2
    Be or Not to Be... 3
    The Tunnel of Vision.. 4
    An Open Torn Heart 5
    Cut 7
    The Howl 8
    Stranger 10
    Listen To the Music 12
    Knowing Comes from Experience......................... 13
    The End... 14

The Mind 2013 15
    Numb 16
    Light 17
    Without an Observation 18
    Barrier ~ 19
    The Mind 20
    The Hallways of a Painted Mind 22
    Memories~ 23
    Cyrus... 24
    No Reconciliation ~ 25
    Parallel Universes—... 26

Dividing Line 2014 27
Perplexed Passion 28
So So 29
A Desultory Mind 30
Dividing Line 31
The Endless Circle 32
An Overlooked Heart 33
The Endless Sea 34
The Footfalls of Wind 35
Ambiguity of Light 36
Gibberish 37

An Untouched Heart 2015 38
Under Way 39
¿? 40
IF 41
Weeping Willow 42
An Untouched Heart 43
Hands of Knives 44
Behind a Veil 45
Swimm 46
When Death comes knocking at your door 47
I have a Voice inside my Mind- it will not let me be 48

Concluded 2016 49
Just Another Circus Clown 50
Ravenous 51
Concluded. 52
Whenever I open my mouth to speak 53
A Fraction of Time 54
Cauldron 55
My Mind, Raped 56
A Tunnel That Loops 57
But you know it, don't you? Every day, day in and out, you sit and think what's the point. 58
Nestle an Eel 59

The Nameless 2017 60
When the Mind awakens 61
Like I 62
The Nameless 63
Constraint 64
Inosaint 65
Noctifera 66
Tell The Sun not to Rise 67
Whatever is This Life 68
Doeyed 69
Bird Whistle 70

Waonderer 2018 71
Waoderer 72
Fragmenting to Null 73
Wearing Tears 74
Friendless Fool 75
The Fate of Us All 76
Sorrowful Widow 77
Uniquely the Average Sheep 78
Writings on the Wall 79
I wonder if we are like stars that drift 80
Luciferian Dreamonic 81

non audeo 2019 82
My Subconscious, She Sneers 83
Foolish is I Who Dreams 84
The Setting Sun 85
Dear My Existence, I Apologize 86
Solar Lives 88
The Words Heard 89
Falling Into Me ~ Parallel Universes 90
They Look, I Mistook 91
non audeo 92
Into the Void, Bitter Soul 93

Never Mine 2020 94
My Secret Sorry Soul 95
The Twisted Truth 96
Written by Time 97
The More I Dwell 98
A Poet's Beating Heart 99
Bring in the Children.. 100
Never Mine... 102
Obligate my Soul 103
Contrived.. 104
There is this senseless void 105

I Wish to Stay Underground 2021 106
She Despaired 107
I Wish to Stay Underground 109
See You in the Mourning... 110
Your words are toxic but I am stronger 111
In me sits a notion 112
I Wish to Delete I 113
I walk along the nightmare of a dream............................... 114
I dug a moat around my heart... 115
Him... 117
Strung Upon these Broken Bones 118

On the Brink 119
Love Less.. 120
Empty Fate.. 121
Wings 122
The Deathbed of Despair: A Fool's Promise 123
I oft think to run away 125
I oft wonder who I am 126
I bounce a penny in my brain.. 127
Grave 128
I fell to dream in fitful turns.. 129

Caught by a Dream 130
Where Art My Marrow... 132
Trapped in a Wish 133
My One & Only 134
Permeate.. 135
Crazy We Crave 136
For Once 138

POETRY KRISTINE HOPE

The Storm 2012

The Storm

1-16-12
Slowly falling down
Beneath thy smile a broken frown
The bright in one's eyes
Shades over and dies
Silence covers thy mouth
Drawing mind to a forbidden south

Ears strain to listen
All that's heard Is words of sin
Hands reach for the star
Though seem too far

Clouds of sin fog one's vision
Shielding warmth of bright sun
Thy blood runs cold
Smiling warmth no longer taking hold
Words of fear scar thy tongue

Spitting venom at those minds yet young
Dark clothing drapes thy skin
Fading away from kin
Cries not seen clouds thy eyes
The you that once was dies

Watching as old dreams fade
Thy believe this must be paid
Is this thy end?
Or will thee find a friend?
To share the thoughts that kill
Surely this must be thee will?

Be or Not to Be

4-18-12

Watching with eyes filled with fear.
Listening with ears clogged with sin.
Waiting for desires oh so selfish.
Grieving the past and present.

Understand others ways, but one's own are lost in the shadow of darkness.
Seeing others with no judgement, but with oneself many.
The path of suffering is followed.
Will thy ever see the light of day?
How will thee see one's wrongs and look at them as indifferent from others?
Can one find oneself fully so thy can help others do the same?

Who am I?
Why are we?
Is this the question?
Or is it more like: why are we so judgmental, critical, selfish fools?

Or are we?
Could it be that there is no true Right and Wrong?
That one is one because there is no reason not to be?
We are looking for ourselves, when we should just be.
To succeed is to fail.
To fail is to succeed.
We are energy whose ends are beginnings and beginnings which never end.

We are who we think we are, and we are not.
Remember this if you wish, or remember it not.
It's up to you to decide.
Be or not to be.

The Tunnel of Vision

5-22-12

Brown eyes stare with intensity

Clouded vision of grey

Looking for immensity

Not knowing what I should say

Eyes are locked

I turn away

I am shocked

I must run away

Will the silence ever be heard?

Or am I lost forever

I can't stand this pain

I am but a bird

With broken, torn wings a sever

I don't see what I'll gain

I am in a world of darkness

A flame so small burns

Abide with helplessness

When will I take my turn?

POETRY KRISTINE HOPE

An Open Torn Heart
7, 2012
My heart is torn
I can only warn
The blood is too deep
I'm afraid I can't sleep

Will I ever find true love?
As beautiful as a dove
Time can only tell
Then I will finally be well

Dreams of desire
Cloud my perception of who to admire
A strong soul is what I need
To take the lead

Hand in hand we Would walk
Silence only broken by necessary talk
Smiles so warm
An unbreakable bond beginning to form

The love is there
I just need to know how to get near
For I can't see
In a shadowed, deserted lea

POETRY **KRISTINE HOPE**

I just need one seed to sow
In time I will let it grow
No need for rushing things
Slowly but surely happiness will bring

But until then I will wait
Behind these cold iron locked gates
You can't bend the bars or break the chains
Only with the key I will be fain

So here I stand all covered in grey
And will always be so waiting for that fine day
A day of happiness it will be
A love so true between him and me

Cut

9-1-12

A small, sharp blade against thy skin

The blood beneath, breaks to the surface and spreads.

A thick deep red oozes out, smothering the thin tip of the blade.

A faraway stare watches thy own arm,

thoughts scarred and betwixt with reality and insanity.

Guilt overwhelms, and a feeling of welcoming the pain in surfaces.

Numb and bitter.

This is to be deserved, this is the payment for what thee done wrong.

When will thee find thyself again, lost in the shadows of death.

Cut thy surface to its beneath; beneath, where the Demons lay infesting and overcoming.

Beware of the bitter sweet smile.

It is not thee.

The Howl
9, 2012

A silent cry escapes the lone wolf,
So distant and aloof-

Her eyes wary and fearful,
She Roams the dank night careful.

Her life crashed into a million pieces,
Like a car into a solid wall.
Her joy forever ceases,
Found Unknown to all.

Hollow and faceless.
Follows the faithless.
Wallow in senselessness.

A world seemingly bliss,
Was never imagined to be as horrid as this.

She can't fathom her arrogance,
How could she have overlooked such a lie-
Her and shameful dance;
Painful thoughts scar her Shy.

Invisible she is to the world.
And the world to her is unfathomable.

A lie was life
The truth turning her to a knife;
But she will do nothing but fight,
For her desires are still out of sight.

Her cries never to be seen,
she knows what that'll mean-
Suffering Alone in silence.
Her smile not revealing her distance.

Stranger

2012

My eyes

They wander over the creatures around me

Through the people I love

And the ones I regard on the street

But is there any

Difference?

My ears

They strain to hear what cannot be

The crowded streets kick and shove

Ones who I will never meet

But an arm brushes an arm

And two humans lock eyes

For that split second there is a connection

Just a spark of light

Maybe it is just a charm

That makes us evaluate our ties

We all can show affection

Though we may as well take flight

"A stranger to all I am

And to all strangers they are to me."

POETRY   KRISTINE HOPE

Take a look at yourself

And see if this is true

A soft helpless lamb

Running in glee

It is what makes the self

And the action that follows too

But what Is the difference?

The lamb is soft on the outside

Beneath though could lay a Darkside

A stranger

The danger

POETRY

Listen To the Music

2012

Time and circumstances.

What causes this?

The mind.

A powerful element; it judges its own actions and acts accordingly.

Everyone acts by thoughts, shards of the mind itself.

We think, constantly think.

But if we'd just stop and watch:

You'd see life acting before itself,

And realize its inevitable mistake-

We never live in the moment.

And because of this our futures are always repeating in the same melody.

A tune so bitter, yet so oblivious.

POETRY KRISTINE HOPE

Knowing Comes from Experience

12-8-12 18:22

And so the day settles

A breath of life releasing its grips

Eyes once before bright with light,

Are covered in darkness again.

"What did one learn today?" Thy wonders. And so it may be that

one thinks they have learned none at all, but we are always learning-

Even in our Dreams.

So as night ignites thy eyelids

And one's mind falls into the turmoil, and roams around one's thoughts

He forgets himself for a moment~ but just for a moment.

A new day awakens,

And thy is feeling fresh and New,

Like a summer breeze, soft and gentle...

And one wonders;

"What is it that thy'll learn today?"

The End

1-5-13

Today was the end of the world

At least that's what they say

But to me it ended long ago

To me it was just the same death row

POETRY   KRISTINE HOPE

The Mind 2013

POETRY

Numb

1-5-13 23:26

The essence of the self is lost

In a dank, void, abyss

Oh how pricy the cost

She surely will be missed~

POETRY KRISTINE HOPE

Light

2-9-13 15:03

Light as a feather

Airless as a cloud

The whisper in the wind,

The silent breath before Dawn~

It's The faceless, hollow stillness

The ghost, the Spirit

The unseen, the unfelt, the unheard of

Invisible, yet watching

Inaudible, yet listening

Fear, as dark as night:

As Voiceless as Light

POETRY

Without an Observation

2-9-13 18:40

The mindless roam the streets

They are so hard to avoid

Try not to look them in the eyes

For they are senseless voids

Their anger gets the best of them

And they never have a thought that is true

So be careful with your manner, and hope that this beast isn't you

Barrier ~

2-15-13 10:05

I lost a person today

Another one gone away

Through the seeds of time

The unkempt dime

Unknown, undefined, as silent as sight:

The hands are bound too tight,

I can't breathe, I can't see

And yet you tear it all away from me

The torture in my mind is dwindling though

It is time to let you go

I am not your fun, I am not a tool

What you have cursed unto me was beyond cruel

I now stand tall, voiceless yet loud

And I call off your infliction, I shall not whimper nor fall

I am strong, you are weak-

It is time I rise to my peak

Hear me now oh Devilish beast, monster so discrete!!

 I am courage in my fear,

 And it is thee that shall endure forevermore!!

The Mind

4-3-13 17:50

The mind is such a mysterious place

Shifting and turning

From the masked face

To the emotional yearning;

A laughing storm

To the thundering warn-

Am I the only present one

Looking past all the fun,

Seeing everyone holding a Gun;

This is where my fear resides,

This is where my mind declines,

This is how it all went down,

That fateful day when the truth was found.

The truth, is youth is a lie, and everything is bitter and cold,

And that No one can hold,

A gun so that it might,

Not end up in a fight;

Dim this if thy wish-

Make this fact unseen to thy eyes, sweet ignorant fool.

But then thy will miss,

All the experience of holding this tool:

This tool, this key, or knowledge as you may see,

Is only for them who need-

Who needs something more,

To take this tour,

Of a place called life,

So fragile and full of strife-

With this knowledge thy shall endow

And show them how-

And then maybe they will drop their weapons,

Of knives, guns, and intentions,

And maybe then they too will know,

Of the Truth of Youth and all that has become-

So then may we swift, and change are view, to not one on one but only one in two.

The Mind is The Truth and the Truth is of Youth and the Youth is a Lie;

Does this knowledge then defy?

The Hallways of a Painted Mind

5-26-13 23:00

Shredded sheets fly through the brisk night window

The concrete glass shatters, pieces scattering in an empty room~

The doors are closed, yet a shadow still walks through

The witch calls out, but she does not conquer:

The hallway is dark, there is no music

The shadows grow, the voices gone

A heart, floating in tears, is on the bedroom floor;

The wolves howl, and the birds sleep

The corners of the sleepy mind awaken,

The voices echo off the white walls,

The bed is on the ceiling,

The music is rewinding;

The witch is returning~ running, running, running; the clouds dance, the ring drowns, the tree explodes.

The beach is blood, the tears dried, the glass is full.

The knife in one hand, the heart in the other, hands stained red: she drinks the blood and smiles.

Words from her forehead, with four eyes...

The ghost in the mirror, the reflection floating on dim light; the light, fading into the background of swings and roller coasters.

The water rises, the tide pulls back.

The face is gone, and in its place is a shadow~ the shadow walks through the doors.

POETRY — KRISTINE HOPE

Memories~

6-5-13 07:03
Today is just a day
Another dream gone a fray,
A thought of life,
Scarred and Stained-

But who am I anyway?
Who is it that walks the streets in search of something;
In search of anything, everything-

Am I just a memory,
Floating on eternity,
With knowledge so precious,
A mind so cautious;
And an existence so
Dull?

Who am I, who am I, who am I-
Am I just here,
To learn and to love and to be,
Close to the ones who are near?

But what if I want more,
What if I have given up this chore-
I'll scream my lungs out so that one might,
Hear me in my flight-

A memory is all I am,
A memory of knowledge so dull,
A mind so full,
And a love so damn.

POETRY

Cyrus

7-12-13 14:05

Why does the Wind blow?

So powerful, then slow,

Wild and frightening- brought on with lightning.

Why does it move, through the trees-

Whispering through the leaves.

Does it have something to say?

Does it have something to convey?

No one knows why the wind blows;

Like an ocean it flows,

Gentle, friendly- harsh, strong;

 'Tis everywhere this wind belong.

No Reconciliation ~

8-2-13 01:11

It is One in the morning,

And I can Still hear your voice.

Ringing in my Mind,

As I take one last sip;

The Poison I drink,

Was brought on by you;

I can't think,

Of nothing But you.

I needed something,

To replace your Memory~

But I can't seem to find,

Anything worthwhile.

All I can do is,

        Think of You...

Parallel Universes—
8-14-13 10:59
I dreamed a dream,
Where my imagination did more than beam,
Where little creature roamed the streets,
The pitter-patter of insect feet.

I dreamed,
That I had feared,
That the man I loved,
Would walk away.

I dreamed of pain so real
I dreamed of Him standing right here,
I dreamed that he hated me.
And that was how it would always be.

I dreamed of bleeding eyes
Of icy cold lies
Dreamed of fire that burned
And I now remember what I had learned;
He didn't love Me.
He didn't need Me.
He wanted Her,
And I could bare it no longer--

I screamed, a blood-curdling scream, in that dream I had dreamed;
I had loved a hater.
I had loved a killer.
 I had loved my lover; or so I dreamed.

POETRY   KRISTINE HOPE

Dividing Line 2014

Perplexed Passion

5-12-14 17:18

There is something frighteningly different from pleasure and peace.

One is a gut-deep demonic hunger, a gluttonous suffocation: driven by the mind.

The other a calm, friendly caress, neither hungered nor thirsted for, but welcomed like it was awaited for in many long tiresome years: driven by the spirit.

So So

5-23-14 20:08

I am so not here, so in space,

In stars... Wandering, wondering;

River flowing, never knowing.

Agitated, complicated.

Caged freely, flying chained.

Conundrum, complication.

I am so not me, so in tune,

In moon... Wondering, wandering;

River flowing, Always knowing.

A Desultory Mind

5-26-14 06:45
I'm not crazy, I'm fucking insane.
Break me, hate me, but you can't make me.
Fucked in the brain, fucked up, fucked in and out.
Thinking clear, thinking sharp, thinking deadly-sharp.
Am I evil, or just mad?
Am I bad, or just sad?
Damned, cursed, or ill.
I've gone so far down the rabbit-hole, now, I can't even tell.

It's ok though, I'm alright.
Just need something, anyone, to fight.
To bite.
With teeth and claws, ripping flesh-
A bloody mess.

Oh, I don't mean to kill.
I am not that far ill.
But I have a strange apprehensive hunger,
Of what for, what of, I can't quite grasp no longer.
But what does it matter.
I'll only become madder.
And madder- yet gladder.

Great. Fantastic. Fine.
These are just a few words I say to emphasize
That I'm alright.
This is the meaning behind these lies,
The truth in disguise;
I am a raging-storm,
A swirling mess of black thoughts, I warn-
Evil, crazy, insane; a loon.
A delusional, illusional, muse.

Dividing Line

5-26-14 15:20

A vivid bloodbath between Morality and Insanity-

Pressured. What is even right?

Kill, conquer, die, relinquish.

What; a strife between two minds.

When will I cross the line?

Which will I go to; love, hate-

Evil, good.

Torn between; standing in the middle.

Both sides are screaming for me to join them.

Why not, stay still…

Tortured Mad.-

The Endless Circle

7-22-14 12:05

Thinking about all that is and could never be.

Believing all is what it is and nothing unwanted will ever leave.

Hoping I am wrong and everything is just a nightmare of a dream.

Being nothing of what I am rather of who others deem.

Doing what they want and not what I want to be.

Thinking about all that is and could never be.

An Overlooked Heart

8-1-14 13:23

Heartbreak, heartache

Hate, hate, hate.

Misinterpret

The actions culprit.

Let live the for-scene,

Forgive, forget, forever.

Why live in regret, moreover.

The heart sighs a silent sigh,

For its intentions were just shy

Of following through to its actions.

Misinterpret

The actions culprit.

Lie, lie, lie.

Heartache, heartbreak

The Endless Sea

9-10-14 22:01

- Sometimes I feel as if I'm floating on an endless sea where I come from nowhere and head toward the vast unknown.

The only sense of direction being the stars and the sun...

    Constantly shifting their own ideas, leading me further into the unknown

  than if

    there were no guide.

The silence surrounds my mind but my thoughts are bombarded by the pull and push of the stars and sun.

  ~ The unknown leading the lost;

the blind leading the blind-

    Children leading children.

The Footfalls of Wind

11-17-14 22:59

In the half-light of night

Through the air the sprits speak

Whispering, whirling;

 Taunting, twirling

Through a frigid land so bleak

Ambiguity of Light

11-22-14 21:26

Light, speckled in its Darkness

Intertwining,

So-ambiguous;

So-mysterious,

Interwinding;

Dark, speckled in its Lightness

Gibberish

12-5-14 21:17

My thoughts, circling.

My mind, hurting.

Will it ever end?

I try to speak my mind, but it seems my lingo is lost on the ears of every passerby.

Can I only speak with cryptic text?

Why, thoughts, do you deter me so!

Such a quandary, a confined space, with no mercy.

I can't break free.

No matter what I do, no matter how I say it, it's always the same.

Lost in the Limbolic nature of my mind.

Do you understand, or is this, too, undefined?

POETRY   **KRISTINE HOPE**

An Untouched Heart 2015

POETRY   **KRISTINE HOPE**

Under Way

3-4-15 05:32

I am drifting away,

 Further,

    Farther,

        I am shoved under way

A life so mundane.

Tick tick ticking away at the seeds of time: they glitter, they flare, then disappear.

¿?

3-28-15 16:20

¿? Question Mark, why do you? Question every little thing you

Think you know

But then you realize you Don't know

    And so try to find a reason why

Why why

Even if there is no answer? To the Question we all seek

Even if there is no reason

    Why

        Why

          Why

We still love a little bit of

Question ¿ Marks

IF
4-1-15 10:14
What if I say
    What if
        What if I say
Everything that's
            On my mind?
What if I yell
    What if I
        What if I yell
 Everything that's
      Torturing me
             Still?
Would you
    Understand
 Would you
    Know what I mean
Would you
    Could you
Tell that I'm
    Slowing going
           Insane?
Would it
    Matter what
        I say
Would it matter
        At all
Should you just
    Could you just
Ignore my every
            Fault?

Weeping Willow
5-2-15 20:02
Weep weep willow tree
Sun kissed leaves swaying free
Weep weep willow tree
Sky alight with the sun's ascent
Owls hoot their mournful songs
As soulful birds make descent

Weep weep willow tree
The sky sheds color as beautiful as thee
Weep weep willow tree
Ominous clouds strike the sky
Suddenly lightning passing by
Thunder shakes the innocent ground
As silent as whispers and then pound pound pound

Like a heart palpitating
Boom boom boom
The sky so crazed it fumes

Fire red light ablaze
Weep weep willow tree
The sky strikes madly down on thee
Weep weep willow tree
Set afire from the turmoil of the storm
Forlorn Forlorn
Cry cry willow tree
Burning burning; crack
No light so bright as a burning willow
In the deep of dark black bellows
Crying pitifully
Weep weep willow tree

An Untouched Heart

5-18-15 21:19

If I gave my heart to you,

Would you know what to do?

Would you know to give it back,

Throw it at me like it's made to lack,

Would you know to stomp on it,

Crush it fast before it makes a fit?

Yes, yes!

That is what you must do

You must you must

Tear my heart in two

For if you're not quick

Never again will my heart go tick-tick

Hands of Knives
5-18-15 22:00
What is love but a torture-device
A thing that holds-fast
And never lets go
Yet it has a strikingly sharp grip
Like hands made of knives
Love is like a torture-device
So cruel to love another
And have them throw your heart away
Like it was nothing
Just another heart of the millions of hearts
To crush
How can I let myself love?
To love is so easy
Free flowing, as natural as can be
I could give my Heart away,
But then it will be locked in your hands- forever
I cannot give my Heart away,
When I know love is a torture-device!
I can love with a beat beat beating
To dim the mounting expanse of
Loneliness- loneliness, like a vast empty, snow field- a land so bleak and cold
But then I'd be burning in a rage rage raging fire,
A wild, erratic cage of fear and desire
The chains that bind me are my own doing,
How can I how can I
Love
When I know
Love is a hateful word.

Behind a Veil

8-21-15 13:01

Foreign words,

Foreign faces,

My Heart spins wild

In Unknown places.

Every bubble shields

A person in a veil

What is beneath

The surface, it creeps

Soundless

Frightful

Stare

through Eyes

Undecipherable lies

Mind spins Frantic

Danger Danger- Diabolic

Vulnerability

Please~ Don't look at Me

Foreign words,

Foreign faces,

My Heart stops

In Unknown places.

Swimm

9-13-15 20:53

Vivid, sweaty, hot body- liquid oozing, wet inducing, oh so woozy heat- Indeed, silent plea, to unbind my knees, and enter me~ passion, frenzy, flee~ palpitating glee! Anticipation hurries south, never could amount, as haunting as this hunt- Cupid, mercy, Wolf- blood and pain is sure; too pure: not at all! Innocence is as children be, and I the horrid wretch~ come tame my ruined heart, or say Goodbye to Me!

POETRY
KRISTINE HOPE

10-11-15 21:48

When Death comes knocking at your door

Like Leaches, it implores

Let it in, and End is sure

Bade it off, and It will

                Knock Down the Door

POETRY

11-8-15 09:32

I have a Voice inside my Mind- it will not let me be

Whispers in my Ear, a silent reverie

I try to Tame the voice, but it would rather tame Me

And I fear, as I Listen, maybe He is Me

Concluded 2016

Just Another Circus Clown

1-13-16 21:14

Feet squandering

  Fucking Wandering

Around and Around

Like a Circus that won't End

  No matter how hard I try

To begin Again

My Face slams into the same imminent

Wrestler

Of Words and Thoughts

That takes Hold,

In a jolt,

   Like a Hook

In a Fish

  Only to Give In

To the Pull

And the Tug

     Of something beyond Control

Ravenous

1-23-16 15:14

I just want someone to Understand- Understand

Just want Him to hold my hand,

And tell me everything will be fine-

Maybe a simple kiss;

    Oh, how I wish!

The pain, builds higher

 Stronger than Desire --

    I wish for it

    It tortures, in a fit

    I can't stop, I need this fix

Please, all I want is you to Care

So that I will Dare

    To Love you Back

 Even if, even if you Lack

The Will

      To Love me too~

I don't care,

All I want-

All I want-

Is Air to breathe~

    I'm suffocating,

In my own Nightmare.

Concluded.

1-26-16 21:46

Have you ever felt so Angry, you felt your eyes may Pop? Smash your head against the wall, if only to feel something, anything, at All.

Have you ever felt so Sad, that tears won't even come, and yet your eyes pain from the Pressure- so Sad, that not even Death Cheers.

So fearful, that Heart palpitation is a shadow, and whispers of thoughts eroding the Mind Away-- so very scared, that Eyes scar the Mind, and Speak eluded.

So confused, so lost- that memories, dreams, and thoughts become one- until what is and what isn't is blurred, and Nothing is Real, not even you, not I, and nothing that has ever Been.

Have you ever felt so Intense, so Filled with Longing and Fiercely of what can never be- that the Mind becomes obsessed, certain, training to one Idea-- and that Idea, Pure Insanity?

Have you ever felt All That, at once, without stopping, without Comfort- just coming and coming, until you feel as though you make break, as the snapping of a Pencil- or neck.

I have felt all Those things, and I Continue to Feel. And I can't take it, anymore. On and Off, on and Off, like a fucked up record playing a song about a Screwed up World that will always be as is, no matter what. And to what Purpose? Answer- billion reasons- for every person alive- answer-- and yet none, hold True, to the Inevitable Conclusion.

POETRY   KRISTINE HOPE

2-10-16 12:34

Whenever I open my mouth to speak

It's like my Veins become inflame

And in it like flight

Tearing at the seems

Excited, Blighted

  A mess of Caustic Poison

Somewhere, here

I am lost, in Mute fear~

Heart Beats

Fumbled Speech

Eyes Fleet

    Toxicity

        From Talk

    A Tonic, if Not~

POETRY   KRISTINE HOPE

A Fraction of Time

3-31-16 20:56

Why, am I, here?

 Why, are you, here?

Together, we, enstrangle--

in a deluded hemisphere.

Cauldron

7-12-16 11:36

Creepy crawling down my spine

Thoughts tangled, shuttered mind

Like a spider, teeth to pinch

Like an itch, I can't scratch

Like the devil, in a laugh

POETRY

KRISTINE HOPE

9-18-16 15:13

My Mind, Raped

  By Words that Patronize

I, contorted, smile and nod

  While, beneath, I'm fuming

With an Unkept Rage

  Kindled by your Ignorance;

And yet, I buckled, beneath the weight

        Of Words

And now, I struggle, between Obey:

  And Answer to None.

A Tunnel That Loops

11-15-16 14:57

What's worse: an unkept fire or stifling bitterness? As much as I... But no...

They are equally horrid.

Here I am, regretting my choice. Did I cause more harm than good? If given it again, I'd done the same as I did.

So no. I can't regret what is already said and done.

But, now, sitting alone with my loneliness, letting it Fester...

I wonder why my soul wakes, every morning still.

I wonder why my soul wakes.

  I wish it would just float away.

Back to wherever it came from...

My soul is cursed.

My life is cursed.

And I... I'm tired of caring.

I'm tired of feeling.

Distraction doesn't work, anymore;

Feelings are like Pins,

 impossible to ignore.

I am so very Lonely. And I don't care...

What am I to do with My Life?

I've no Drive Left.

I've nothing left.

Somewhere, somehow, it was slowly snuffed out.

All I am now, is a dark candle sitting on a dusty shelf.

Without use.

No more memories to share in.

No more Light to be had.

Just dark, cold, listless...

The Sordid Wolf has finally lost her way,

And the Hopeless Hoper no longer

Hopes.

POETRY

KRISTINE HOPE

11-17-16 23:23

But you know it, don't you? Every day, day in and out, you sit and think what's the point.

Down in a cave, you fumble forward, reaching for something in the darkness when you know very well there's nothing there. Only the dampness of the air, the sickness in your stomach, walls and darkness. And yet you reach, and reach and reach, and as you go further and further down doubt picks up and rolls you around, and you scream and scream for help, even as you know there is no way anyone could possibly hear you, so buried deep underground. And then you find yourself, turning in mad circles, pulling out your hair, and beating the walls with your fists until you can taste the blood in the air.

And then, nothing. You stand, motionless, thoughtless, staring unseeing at the wall, nothing left to do...

Except, start again.

Day in and day out.

POETRY   **KRISTINE HOPE**

Nestle an Eel

12-26-16 00:35

Nothing ever comes to comfort me

Except silence and darkness

Silence and darkness

And Fear

Ever echoing

Ever echoing

In the enclaves of my Mind

The Nameless 2017

When the Mind awakens
the Soul is trapped
by the World

1-19-17 18:25

To spend my days in mostly uninterrupted solitude. As we are all like wolves, communal in our ways, I can imagine it's hard for some to see one so content with being on her own. But I do better alone. I always have. In the hustle of busy mouths only my mind remains awake. I wonder if their minds are sleeping? Even as I try to escape the world I live in, it seems I'm the only one who has ever been here. Being the one among so very many who convulses at the thought of playing such a superficial game. I cannot.

My heart gets the best of me.

Like I

3-2-17 16:12

Always in the background

Cast in Shadow

Listening to others talk

Watching as others fall in love

Always the Outcast

Never apart of the Circle

Talking Dull; Thinking Dark

Pushing people away

Sitting Alone, Walking Listless

Wondering if there is,

Out There,

Another Lost Soul like I

The Nameless

3-28-17 13:10

Like the slinking beast of Schrödinger

My head both dead and not

   Though, feeling less here

Like my world is just pages from a book

And the edges are blurring,

From the dreams that seep beneath

From a Mind Kept Turning,

   Twisted and Churning,

Of Bloody Thoughts and Tortured Hearts

A Hell Beyond a Hell

               A Life Beyond the Living

Constraint

4-24-17 17:15
It does not matter
what you say or don't say
It all ends up the Same.

I look at myself, and see nothing.
I look at myself, and feel nothing.
Who Am I, even?
Blank faces stare; my Mind, wondering,
What are you Thinking of me of This?

Does it matter? Do I Matter?

How am I to get to know another soul when I don't know where mine is.
Each day ticks away...
Footsteps beat to the tick of the clock, while I, delirious, fumble along.

In all serious petty sadness, what is the point of my dismal existence? I do nothing but fear and vent and vent and fear!
I might as well be fear itself, whispering in other's ears of the demons people try to ignore.

I do nothing, I say nothing, I am nothing.
No action is seen unless acted;
No thought responded to unless expressed;
Nothing in return if nothing given.

Maybe I want nothing of the world...
Oh, if only I knew that but even I don't know what I want!

But again, again, again...
What does it matter? What do I...
Matter.

Nothing but a substance taking up space.
Nothing but nothing living life at its petty pace,
recognized by others only as a pretty face.

It does not matter
what you say or don't say
It all ends up the Same.

Inosaint

5-25-17 23:43

Lonely hearts gravitate

To my spontaneity

But they do not realize that,

Beneath the surface,

 I'm a wretched fiend.

One that,

   Draws you in,

Like a current,

   And sends you out to sea ~

With nothing left but,

A broken fantasy

Noctifera

6-26-17 19:43

Insanity is not Evility -

Though Darkness taints

The Insane,

  They are ever the Innocent;

Only when The Dark devours

      The Saint

Does the True Madness

            Smile

Tell The Sun not to Rise

9-28-17 00:21

"You are not messed up, you chose to do that. Simply don't."
It's as simple as not to do,
Is it, Mr. Helper?
It's as simple as forget it,
Is it, Mrs. Angel?
Tell that to an alcoholic,
  Who's spent their Life
Wanting;
Tell that to a suicidal,
Who's spent their Life,
Hurting;
Wherever have I been,
Wandering and Wondering?
Whatever am I for,
Squandering and plundering,
Peoples Heats and Minds?
I am, destined, to be alone;
You say simply don't.
I've spent my life,
        Breaking.
Just as the ocean, against the cliffs;
Just as the earth buckles beneath;
Just as my life, drama never to cease;
Like the cataclysm of an Avalanche,
Just as lakes form from glaciers,
The lava raging from volcanos,
Fires that ravage the forests,
And hurricanes that never cease
      destruction.
Just simply don't, try it, tell nature to not mind it's nature!
Tell me, again, to simply not!
No you! Simply knot my heart and cast it aside, away, asunder, adrift~
    Where It, Breaking, Belongs.

Whatever is This Life
10-9-17 19:28

Who needs sleep?

        Ha!

  Who needs, eat?

Formulating a conundrum I

  Can't surpass

Realizing my reality is

  What Is

Circling around my Ill-Minded

        Life

What Of strife!

    It makes me bleed on the inside,

    It makes me bend on the inside,

  Trying and Fighting,

Hardly much of a Goal in mind;

To Think, To Feel~

        What's Real?

Battling against the current,

  But it laughs, so sardonically

        As I sink deeper;

  I can't help it- Still, I Struggle, Bereft

Doeyed

10-29-17 23:28

Dismayed, enraged, out of range-

Dismayed, enraged, in a cage-

My mind seems to pop and snap

  Little cells withering away

  Little lives tethered to mine, wasted

What am I doing Here?

Numb, cold, lost- no Voice

Stringent, struggle, faltering- Vice

     Where is Victory in This?

Everything blurs as time moves ever onward, and I, like a deer, simply stand

       Dismayed

POETRY

KRISTINE HOPE

Bird Whistle

11-22-17 12:23

Through a field of dreams and down a kaleidoscope of nightmares I wander and wonder about the infinitesimal nature of life as it hurries across battlefields to a never ending void of gray clouds and slithering teeth while I on the sideline beg to stay behind because I cannot stand it when claw meets claw and would much rather grapple with the wolf that knows my name and the fox that told me so and building chaotic structures in the sky as if I were some superhuman creator or some kind of queen.... The Goddess of Night

POETRY

KRISTINE HOPE

Waonderer 2018

POETRY

Waoderer

7-7-18 20:14

Wandering around

the shores of my mind,

I see, but cannot define ~

A mirage, a hope, the delusion of this Soul's confusion ~

   a figment of any mare,

         yet, Never There --

Oh, how wonderful is this

Wondering anguish

Fragmenting to Null

8-30-18 15:33

There have been many a word

That appear

    Awaken Worlds

Then dissipate

    Seeping back into

        whence they came

Before there is a chance

        To fuel their flame

        Ink their madness

        Bind them to page

Wearing Tears

9-3-18 02:37

I wear my face as it hurts to wear it

I wear my Soul as it aches;

   I wear my Heart as it fades~

I wear my name as others have it...

      I wear out my Mind

           As it wears its own

           Face, Name

           Heart, Soul

           And it does not

                  hurt,

               ache,

                  or fade;

And Others Haven't it.

Friendless Fool

9-7-18 15:01

Leaping to converse like some
        desperate beggar
Avidly engaged with words;
      Then, I remember myself
The sudden realization pulls me back
        To Reality
'Who am I to say Hello?
Does she even realize,
      I'm a Friendless Wolf,
        A Mouse,
        An Outcast.'
Then she sees it,
   For her words stop,
And my eagerness melts,
With each fading silence,
And I begin to wonder the point;
Apt to try again,
I turn to her, but she is Gone;
Tail between my legs, I follow abjectly,
   But Her Friends Crow around Her
And I'm left in the Shadows
Like some Homeless Beggar
Sniveling for Scraps of Words
     Only to be met with Silence

The Fate of Us All

9-23-18 15:05

All of us, shrouded in the darkness of death

It seeps to the surface

Like ink bleeding into the pages of a book;

Alas a book! that will have a beginning, and an end-- a dismal end!

All of us, carry death like a coat

Snuggling against it

Laughing alongside it

Until one day, it rears its ugly head

And growls out its ill-fated Omen:

Alas we're all dead inside!

It eats at us, like some cancerous fiend,

Some knotty little creature

Tip-toeing into our lives

        Smiling, as we Die

Sorrowful Widow

11-5-18 00:00

I am with the night, the dark night, the stars that circle above around and around telling us the same omen about ourselves over and over to countless different people only for them to end up all the same, only for them to fight and to die and to cry only for them to bleed for what for what for love surely and yet they balk from it, cower, like it is some monster, some sort of fiend that crawled from the depths of hell and not the thing that which they most crave

Uniquely the Average Sheep

11-9-18 17:13

Just another person human thing suffering in its own way in a life in a place you will never even be

Writings on the Wall

11-30-18 03:29

I kinda wanna just curl up in a tiny ball and never move again

Find some remote corner where no one will find me

And die a lonely death

Cause no man will ever dare venture where these feet have tread

In this world where feelings are never fed

I, with oh so many, struggle, lost and dead

POETRY

KRISTINE HOPE

11-30-18 04:06

I wonder if we are like stars that drift, yes drift, ever onward, alone, in an endless and vast sea of darkness, in an endless and vast expanse of loneliness

Luciferian Dreamonic

12-23-18 10:33

Tasty little demons are the dreams that entice and torment, that bring you in and laugh in your face as you realize nothing indeed is truly real. Fickle are those dreams, and yet you thirst for them, long for them every waking breath, wait for them to come again. They are unlike any mare or dream, unlike anything ever possible in Reality~ they exist in the realm beneath limbo, where one's reality is so unreal to the point that the unreal is real, yet one's mind is wide awake. Oh, sweet demonic dreams, where will you take me next? My poor tortured mind likes to torment me, play with me~ it knows that which I most crave and yet it keeps it ever so slightly out of my sight. Oh, my mind laughs at me as I stumble forward to meet it, only to find a dark and black void, only to find Myself. Where is He, in this dismal and uncanny fog? Where is my Love, my Life, my Eternal Tormentor? Alas, there is nothing here but an empty mind, nothing here but fragments of a broken soul~ scattering in the wind, never to be seen again. And yet, my mind ever laughs as it weaves the web of my demise.

POETRY   **KRISTINE HOPE**

non audeo 2019

My Subconscious, She Sneers

1-17-19 21:01

She Smirks as one does

Playing with their Prey

Pretending to Ponder the Question

"What does she think of Him?"

And she doesn't even try to Comprehend

The value He holds to Me

Instead She Laughs with those Cynical Eyes,

And Replies:

    "Your Obsession and Demise."

Foolish is I Who Dreams

1-18-19 05:00
the day arises
as the sun sets
where night contends the day
and the moon devours the sky
foolish is I who dreams
careless is I who loves
foolish and careless
heartled and wretched
  Lover of Dreams
night devours the day devours the night
dreams become my day
as I forsake myself for the night
mares
for I belong to them
as they whisper their promises
that they will never ever keep
I belong to they
who will always forsake me
              love me
          and hate me
the night devours the dreams devours the day
if ever a fool 'tis I
  for I've loved and lost within the same breath lostness lover wandering dreams
carelessly hoping
        ever wondering
               as the night devours my mind as my dreams forsake the day
            foolish is I whose lover
Is never what he seems

The Setting Sun

3-12-19 09:41

Sometimes I forget that people die

With the busy of day that clusters our lives

Sometimes, I forget that people die

With each broken promise

Or sorry goodbye

I look towards the sky

And wonder why I

Live a life like it will never end

Live a life, like I have time to love again

Sometimes, I forget that I'm alive

Dear My Existence, I Apologize
3-21-19 16:53

"You say too much,"

    She sneers.

                    I apologize.

"You say too little,"

    He quibbles.

                    I apologize.

"You're too pensive,"

    She remarks.

                    I apologize.

"You're too nice,"

    He announces.

                    I apologize.

        "You talk too much."

"You never give it a chance..."

            "You're too quick to act..."

"Think, don't just do!"
    "Why aren't you ever spontaneous?"
"You will never be enough."
    "Quit trying, and just do something!"
"Why do you always act this way?"
    "You say too much."

Rainbows beatify the world with in its light,
    and I,
Am only ever so sorry for my pitiful plight
Apologizing for my actions and inactions
    In the same breath
Apologizing for my words said and unsaid
    With instant regret
Rainbows beatify the world with its colors,
    and I,
Only see my faults professed by others

    I apologize

    To Myself
For only listening to their words
    It is time that I'm heard
        So sorry
        not sorry
    I say just enough

Solar Lives

6-21-19 11:57

Every human birth accounts for thousands of species lost

Every human heart beating accounts for millions of lives gone

When will human lives mean more than destruction?

When will the price paid for our convenience be enough?

We are willing to take action when our own monuments and buildings go up in flame

What of the forests that are engulfed only for profits sake?

What of the millions of lives lost

For that plastic toy left abandoned

A human's joy means another's suffering —

When have we arrived at this ignorant charade!

Shall we continue to debase the name of the human race, or pave the path to a future that gives instead of

takes and takes and takes

Until there is nothing left

But the rotting corpses of the dead

And the ashes of yesterday

The Words Heard

6-25-19 18:44

No one will care if you're gone
He said
Whispering the words
of the demons in my head
Wondering what I did
Shuddering at my mind, dead
And I said
Why don't you think before you speak
Act before you preach
The lessons that you teach
Are nothing more than bitter words
Of a damned fool
Who doesn't realize the impact
Who only wants you to react
When he says
No one will care if you're gone
And quite frankly
You're wrong
So why don't you go ahead and dare to deny
That it is really my time to shine
If I'm gone
The world will cry and defy
And shout my name as I fade away
For this life is worth it today
And throughout all time
No one will care if you're gone
He said
Whispering the words
I no longer heard

Falling Into Me ~ Parallel Universes

7-11-19 12:09

Falling into daze

Falling into not

Frozen fish and creatures

Falling through the void

Falling through the world

Chaos at the other side

Who am I now?

Mixed ideologies of

Dreamer and Reality

I cannot grasp the truth I want

Lost in the shadow of doubts,

Where people laugh and gawk

Saying I was never meant to be

Her, the savior of their world

   And then I awaken,

   Away from a world of possibility

   To change other's perceptions

   To fly high and mighty

To a reality I will never miss

The next night I find myself

Falling into dreams

They Look, I Mistook

7-19-19 19:59
Clock Ticks
Heart Flicks
They look
 I Mistook
  Misstep
  Mistake
Heat Beats
Fumbled speech
"Well, aren't you perfect."
    Beneath,
My blood is on fire
My pulse a pyre
And my mind,
  Numb
  Mishap
  Muddle
  Mare
Clock Stops
 Mind Dips
They glare
   I Forget
     Fluster
     Falter
Mind Skips
Silent lips
A question hung in air
    To you,
I look so quiet
Perfectly Imperfect
And I wonder,
Should I even be here?
Clock Ticks
Heart Flicks
They look
      I Mistook
         Misstep
            Mistake

non audeo
9-11-19 16:20

I dare not look at people

And therefore I am blind

To every passerby

Who ever walks my way

I dare not speak to people

And therefore I am silent

With every person met

Who ever offers speech

I dare not act near people

And therefore I am unnoticed

By every person here

Who never knows I'm there

POETRY KRISTINE HOPE

Into the Void, Bitter Soul

12-27-19 01:11

I feel like I'm staring into a cold, endless void that I'm wishing would stare back,

but all I feel is a dark expansive emptiness that creeps into my soul

Never Mine 2020

My Secret Sorry Soul

2-13-20 20:54
wishes are like dreams,
they can only fade away

My secret sorry soul
Quickly burned a flame
That can no longer burn

Frozen is my Heart
Frozen is my Heart

We hate ourselves so much
we learn to love another like us,
to fill the void we could never fill

Love is toxic to my Soul
Love is toxic to my Soul

You laugh as love laughs,
For it is so cruel

My secret sorry soul
Yearning for a flame
That will never burn

Let me go
Or I will die

Hopes are like horrors,
Haunting me always

The Twisted Truth

3-26-20 00:37

Sobering the line I walk on,

Muddying the water I drink,

Poisoning the heart I beat with:

The Devil's in the Sink.

Where is the lurid mind,

Beneath the quiet depths?

I want to scream out my mind,

And hide away the inept.

To trust, to trust, to trust

Everything I think I know

And yet know nothing.

I want to bleed my lungs,

I want to bury my bones,

I want to scratch away every part

That has ever made me whole.

Written by Time

3-30-20 14:35

The parts of myself stitched together in an uneven whole,

contemplating the reality of a life not my own,

I wonder if I shall walk the shores of an imagined life,

or step into the world and become what I might?

The uneven elements shift and rest

uncomfortably in the pit of my chest,

a stoic weight while my heart arrest

the snaky veins in a corpse decomposed

the lungs submerged in blood exposed

the shaky feeling of a brain arose

The parts of my soul shattered and melted in jagged whole,

wondering the dream of a death not my own,

I contemplate as I walk the shores of wine,

if I shall step into a world not written by time

The More I Dwell

6-5-20 00:06

The more I dwell on my mind,

The more it drills into me

The more I sit in my shit,

The more I tend to eat

The more my heart rolls around,

The less to bury under ground

A Poet's Beating Heart

9-5-20 11:56

A poet's beating heart
Is nothing but a curse
Let it beat upon my chest
And string along the hearse

I never met a one
Who got more than he gave
For a poet is nothing more
Than slave to his own page

Forgive my sorry soul
I only know one song
And it sings along quite plaintively
For it has buried mirth

I never met a one
Who often sat and spoke
Without the need to write the words
Begging to let go

A poet's bleeding heart
Will always stain the page
A pen to pierce the soul
And send it to the grave

POETRY

KRISTINE HOPE

Bring in the Children
9-11-20 13:02
Waking to pain
Nothing to gain
Hiding the shame

Can't comprehend this world and its intentions
Everyone's so divided it's hard to decide
I'm stuck in the middle looking left and right
Will the world burn or be shut-ins for life?

Waking the hurt
Stifle the mirth
Follow the hearse

Waiting the day the world goes away
Death at least seems peaceful
Wherever I go at least I know it's not
Engulfed in flames and people aren't
Battling their rage

Walking the line
A life not mine
Mind in decline

Honestly my outlook on life is dim
My world was always grim

And now everybody wants to tear down the fragile walls we live in
I can't seem to find a reason to continue it

My heart's a crime
Live poor and die
A life of lies

I feel so hopeless I wish I were never conceived
My parents differ as much as the world it seems
Always picking their battles like it's some kind of game
Well let me tell you something before it gets worse
Before we're all humming this verse

Instead of being united we're all divided
Like it's some kind of contest to see who's the loudest
Like children on the playground we play with our hearts
We play them quite well then tear them apart

Well I call to end the game
To bring in the children and to end the play
Because if the world keeps burning
We might as well call the hearse in

Bury our souls
Borrow the mirth
This world is cursed

Never Mine

9-26-20 01:14, 01:54

I spin a line, I spin a web, and wonder why, I'm in debt

I flip a coin, I drift along, and ponder when, I'm alone

I carry on, a measured mind, and wander where, never mine

I skip a beat, a hapless feat, and flounder here, among my mare

-

I keep in line, I never dare, and thinking there, I'm always scared

I leave today, a hopeless road, and feeling how, I'm in doubt

I get the rhyme, I bid the time, and looking up, among the muck

I weave the lace, a threadbare heart, and shutting down, torn apart

I spool a line, I spew a lie, and wonder where, I'm defined

I find a tool, I am adrift, and finding folly, among the shift

I drop it off, a maddened mine, and wander why, never mind

I beat my heart, a hopeless art, and blinded by, a foolish lie

Obligate my Soul

10-27-20 14:49

And so I commit myself

To the duty of the dull

I apply myself

To compute and recall

I shuffle through the motions

Of a life on call

Remember to punch in

Assigning my life to the clock

And my heart is mute

Tangled among the wires

That twist and strangle

Any feeling left alive

For only the dead accept their fate

And so I must kill my heart

So that I can commit myself

So that I can apply myself

To the duty of the dull

To the life of the dead

POETRY

KRISTINE HOPE

Contrived

12-24-20 09:49, 09:57

1. The way we create happiness like it could ever be manufactured, like some plastic toy on an assembly line that will arrive for a child who plays with it for a day then leaves it in the corner, only for it to be tossed out with yesterday's trash

2. The way you whisper feelings and flaunt love letters like some kind of romantic, though we both know you hate that lovey-dovey stuff and yet you do it anyway, somehow thinking store bought flowers and poems scrawled in half-off Hallmark cards will make any difference to a marriage that has long since been abandoned

3. The way holidays make me feel, all gift-wrapped and tied with pretty decorations, hiding all our scars and shadows, as if plastic smiles and eggnog could mask the feelings of the rest of the year, as if a predetermined day could be spent in joy when the world is falling apart

4. Me, who forgets to be myself sometimes, who forgets that I am a person too and sometimes I do matter, if only a little. Who wraps her life in pretty bows and plastic smiles and fabricated happiness in the hopes that everyone else is at least a fraction happier, only then could I live with the shadows, only then, because at least someone, somewhere, was happy, can be happy, even if that could never be me

There is this senseless void

12-26-20 15:59

There is this senseless void

Where all life shifts and drifts

It never begs to want

Or struggles when amiss

It simply sits and molds

Like the black upon the crust

It simply goes along

Like a boat upon a gust

It never seeks your pain

It has nothing at all to gain

It simply sits alone

Beneath every sun and storm

It wears a face of hope

And flaunts a fragrant smell

Where one does simply wish

That everyone would be well

Yet this is simply life

Living as it does

There is no wonder to the why

Because the answer always lies

It floats along like a leaf

Caught on a summer breeze

And in all the days we're awake

We have no use, it seems

I Wish to Stay Underground 2021

She Despaired

1-25-21 13:34, 13:44, 13:52, 14:43, 15:18

He was a wolf at heart. He stalked the shadowed paths of her mind every evening to look upon the lingering thoughts she had of him. He was indifferent. She was distraught.

>It carries the weight of the wind
>A figment of a life sewn in
>A barrage of words of love and
>Sin, silence screams above the din

She was a shadow in the night. She wandered the forest of his mind alone and shuddered at the demons lurking there. She was frightened. He was thrilled.

>It follows the fear of fated
>A fragrance of loss and hatred
>Destiny of love gone jaded
>Still clinging to life left latent

He was a creature of mares. He threatened to overwhelm her existence with passion and poisonous whispers. She was intrigued. He was satisfied.

It trickles a tainted truth of

Time, torn and worn by worry and

Lies, a deceit painted by a

Promise, left wilting in the dust

She was a ghost among the living. Drifting through her days while dreaming of a life that would lead her heart at the edge of rapture. She was bewildered. He wasn't there.

It whispers silent solace, stuck

Upon her heart, a secret soul

Caressing a mind made maddened

From obsession and delusions

He was a wolf. Haunting her mind, her dreams, her heart. He never was there. She despaired.

I Wish to Stay Underground

3-3-21 11:35

I wish to stay underground

With the voices and the noise

With the demons and the dark

So that no one could ever find

My heart, and tear it apart

Until all my words are insignificant

Until who I was becomes distorted

And left to rot with my body

Nothing more than trash

So yes, I wish to stay underground

Where no one knows my name

Out of light, out of fame

Into the darkness I've claimed

Where my voice is lost

And no one knows I was ever here

Drowning in my mares

See You in the Mourning

3-21-21 23:49
See you in the mourning
When the murder of crows
Eat upon the corpses of doves
And the wings of the phoenix turn to dust
And lay waste to all hope and love

See you in the mourning
Where I'll sit by a coffin
Coated in a darkness of the void
Etched in a stone of eternity
Where all souls will rest
Forgotten to the world
Except for those who wander still
In the graves of the past

See you in the mourning
When the sun rises and the skies are clear
And my heart is cold and alone
When the warmth of the world
Never reaches my soul
And I am left there, wondering
Will it ever end?

See you in the mourning
Before your corpse has hit the ground
Before the coffin is carved
Before we wonder why
Before we say goodbye

See you in the morning

Your words are toxic but I am stronger

4-5-21 22:47

"You bore me," He muttered. It was sudden and cold, with eyes that wandered away like passing stars that never stopped to shine on you, never stopped to bathe you in their warm and eternal glow, telling you how much they adore your worship; alas they wander like the moon wanders across the night sky without any thought to the stars it eats in its path, like the clouds wander when the storm breaks in the heat of Spring. He walks, he walks away then, he walks like the lion walks from the pray it just devoured, like the pray that rots in the sand and is never mourned, the pray that decays and is plagued by fungi and returns to the earth as if it never left, unnoticed and unhurried. Yes, he walks, he walks away like the beast walks, unaware of the damage it has done, unaware of the horror, of the bloodshed, of the torment and pain. He doesn't look back. He doesn't look, like the ocean never looks, it never looks upon the land, the land it eats and eats, the land it sinks beneath its waves until there is nothing left but water, an endless expanse of a raging, indifferent sea, full of monsters that lurk waiting to surface, waiting to drag down to the depths anything and everything. All that's left are the words, the words get caught and linger in the air, drifting, clipping on the ears, slicing, cutting and chopping up the ears, until all one hears are the screams, the screams of your voice, screaming across the mountain range, those glorious wonderful beautiful rocks that will never ever care, that will never ever be there for you to lean on, to be loved by— but never are they ever bored.

Your words are toxic but I am stronger.

POETRY

KRISTINE HOPE

In me sits a notion
4-10-21 13:34
In me sits a notion
It creeps along my spine
It feels beyond recall
I never had it at all
Before, stealing self from mine—

It festers beneath a feeling
I've had it all my life
It often lingers in the shelves
Of my tormented mind

Now there is a newness
I noticed this past year
It often whispers in my ear
Of feelings left to rest

I beg it for a solace
But it simply sits and waits
For what, I do not know—
Only that it's late

Too late for second questions
Too late to wonder why
Too late to rebuild a future
Where I am whole inside

In me sits a notion
It creeps along my spine
I beg it for a solace
From my tormented mind

I Wish to Delete I

4-20-21 09:07

The days pass like a blur and I

Follow the path I declared I

Would never go; and yet here I

Am, stumbling ever onward. I

Forget my soul in order to repay my

Deeds, so that I

Can stifle the longing for something greater

Can force myself to smile, nod, and pay attention to life when in reality, I am slipping

Beneath a facade, a fabricated portrait I

Painted of myself; i

Seem to pretend that i

Matter, when in truth, i

Don't even know who i

Am; who am i

Really? one that walks a path I was given,

One that accepts, obeys, and acts

'Yes, of course, no worries.'

I wish to delete this self that I've created.

I wish to delete the only thing holding me back.

I wish to delete I

I walk along the nightmare of a dream

5-19-21 08:56

  I walk along the nightmare of a dream

  I run towards a life that could never be

  I stumble forward in these dismal feats

  I realize now I am only meant for thee

  I chain myself to the workings of a jaded mind

  I cut off feelings so as to live a lie

  I drive away to see another time

  I want to find the sunrise in this eternal night

  I need to fight this torment in my soul

  I have to find the truth before it's cold

  I thirst for passion before I am too old

  I crave a heart that beats, beats me to a pulp

  I wish to have a me that isn't here

  I hope to find a place where I no longer fear

  You who are always there

  You who feeds me darkness and despair

I dug a moat around my heart

5-26-21 15:39, 17:14

I dug a moat around my heart

And still the knights would leap

So I filled the moat with gasoline

And let it flame beneath

Still the men would fight the fire

And arrive at the iron door

So I got a lion to

Eat them just before

I built a wall around the moat

So as to fend off more

Because they kept coming to my heart

Eager to adore

Still they scaled the wall

The many that were there

To find what lied deep inside

A heart still beating here

I made the castle into a fortress

I dug the moat deeper still

I got some demons and evil creatures

And set bombs beneath the well

I sat before my heart then

Waiting for them to come in

Armed with all manner of things

They will never win

Then there was a silence

It echoed through the halls

It set a weight upon my heart

For no one climbed the walls

No one braved the moat

No one dared the fiends

No one cared to try

For I'd broken all their dreams

And left them out to die

Him.

6-7-21 00:33, 00:46

I painted you with vibrant colors so as to feel
Alive. You came to me inside my dreams and
Whispered only lies. Still I held your heart to
Mine in hopes I'll find you here, by my side
Loving me, until the end of time.

I used a pen without the point, and so you
Were quite dark, the ink it smeared until you
Had, slithered to my heart. Now it stings when I
Bleed, because I loved a ruse, a lie I told myself
When life was blurry and abused.

I carved your soul to my own, so as to feel less
Alone, but it only brought more pain. I sit and
Beg for your embrace, to feel your warmth or
Rage; because you make me whole inside, you
Make me want to fly, to tell the world I'm happy
Now, with you here by my side.

I dug a well for my tears, to fill with all the
Years I spent chipping away at my mind,
Tinkering with all the thoughts inside, trying to
Mend the breaking, not realizing I was making
The recipe for my demise— the truth I've left
Aside to rot so as to not have a day to
Face it.

I wrote a word, and then some more, until the
Strings sewn your life, until the yearning and
The strife, dissolved inside the dream of mine,
A place where mares were mute and fears
Were floating beyond our care, a place where
You and I would be, forever, always,
Written here.

Strung Upon these Broken Bones

6-26-21 20:41, 20:44
To be left alone with your thoughts
To have them pound against your brain
Talking of the things that were
Taunting you with the pain

To see you in a crowd again
To hope to hear your voice
Only for the faces there
To stare without a noise

To be standing at the edge of a cliff
To be screaming my heart out loud
To be asking god what's the point
When there's no one left around

The sinking feeling at the dead of night
When the crickets mourn the day
And you're stuck inside your mind
And then you wish to pray

You hope and plead to a god
You still do not believe
Yet the sinking is so vast
It's all that's left to fake

Then you find you're lost inside
Lost inside a fading mind
Lost among the ghosts and ghouls
A simple, ugly, wanton fool

And then you feel the knowing now
The dreadful truth that the soul somehow
Strung upon these broken bones
Will always be alone

On the Brink

7-23-21 14:56

I need to sort out the files in my mind

To figure out the reason I'm insane

To filter through all the needless mistakes

To find the truth beside this lofty pain

To stop beside the drifting memories

To ask myself why I feel the need

To pick apart the little pieces of my soul

And to leave my heart aside until it molds

Until it grows the ugly things I fear

Until it festers with a feeling I can't bare

Until I'm left with regret and am hungry for

A love of life I've never strived to have before

So I wander through my mind this fickle night

To figure out why I am the way I am inside

To wonder why I never stopped to think

Why my soul is always on the brink

Of Madness

Love Less
8-3-21 10:38
I have this yawning in my stomach
It will not go away
It gnaws upon the walls
And eats and eats the pain

That lingers in my heart
That wormed inside my brain
That I've carried in my soul
The deeds of my mistakes

Yet it feasts upon the yearning
It dulls the fickle aching
It numbs the flame that festers
From a loveless sickly scar

It tears apart my insides
It licks the broken bones
It takes a bite of my organs
Until the hurt is real

Until it stings and burns
Until the stars don't shine
Until the dark is right
Until I'm numb inside
And all these lonely feelings die

Empty Fate

9-4-21 23:16

A quiet creeping apathy has knocked upon my door

I tried to offer tea, though I knew it would abhor

The thought of sweetest in its dark

For it harbors no remark

No twinges in its heart

About anything at all

Instead it sits and waits, for me to claim my fate

To welcome it inside, so I may numb my worried mind

With the feelings of an empty place

Wings

9-14-21 18:05

I once ate the happiness I caught on the wind
It flurried and hurried and sent my heart ablaze
But I clipped my wings and wilted my soul within

I stumbled on a dream of painted promises in plastered grins
I coughed up clovers to cut through the stifled rage
I once ate the happiness I caught on the wind

I weaved a tale of folly in uneven threads
I carved my heart where laid a covet caged
But I clipped my wings and wilted my soul within

I wavered at the sight of deceit seeping threats
I shuddered in the throes of silent shame
I once ate the happiness I caught on the wind

I tiptoed beneath the shadowed secrets sent
To the depths of a muddied mind now maimed
But I clipped my wings and wilted my soul within

It was a time when I rested my soul upon a gift
A life shattered by sinking snake fangs
I once ate the happiness I caught on the wind
But I clipped my wings and wilted my soul within

The Deathbed of Despair: A Fool's Promise

9-17-21 01:42, 01:53

I am at the deathbed of despair,

Sent to wander the purgatory of forgotten dreams.

I wallow in the tears of the yesteryears where I welcomed the home of freedom on the lithe breeze as it carried me towards a peaceful serenity; oh, to be caught on the breeze!

Now I'm marooned at the edge of time, where fate is in the hands of the brave, where I sit and wait for courage to steal my soul and send me out to the distant sea.

And I wait,

And I wait

But the feelings never dissipate; the voice that calls in the dead of night and asks, "What is the life you live?"

And I cannot answer it, because there's a sickly knowing I dare not know, the silent suffering of the self in stagnation.

I dare not name the deed!

The haphazard slew of events that carefully dug out this path for my stumbling feet.

And oh, how they stumble now, now in the sorry footsteps of the one who carried me, once,

So long ago now, a time before I knew.

And I'm seated in the knowing now.

I'm carved upon a life I'm meant to tread,

Wavering, muttering, fumbling in the

Madness of it all, the terror of it all,

The division of us all, together but so far.

And how can I not admit, it's all my fault?

Mea Culpa! Mea Maxima Culpa!

For I am a weak, worn out thing;

I drift as a ship in a storm,

Letting it take me wherever it wants,

Letting it make me leave all that I love.

And I love the taste of freedom

On the breeze— But I've settled on a path

Of the broken and forgotten dreams,

Standing on the precipice of silent screams

Mourning the death of despair—

Because hope is a fool's promise.

I oft think to run away

9-29-21 18:58

I oft think to run away

The thought then clinks against my skull

It points and probs and holds my faults

Its bitter laugh and wanton teeth

Sink their way to my heart

To burrow in my doleful woe

To paint a vibrant lie beneath

And grasp a vice I've woven there

Then flaunt it in the open air

To shame my sickly sorry soul

Until my will has shut the door

And I no longer care at all

I oft wonder who I am

10-7-21 14:46

I oft wonder who I am

I never dared to greet my soul

It laughs a song I've come to know

About a life I hadn't lived

It speaks a language I cannot hear

It splinters with a flagrant fear

And never have I ventured far

Nor as I've sunk beneath the dark

Thought to grasp my spirit lost

In the shadow of a soul I've not

POETRY

KRISTINE HOPE

10-9-21 14:09

I bounce a penny in my brain

And oft I wonder why I'm insane

It tinkers with the thoughts inane

A creeping feeling of the deranged

A smiling mirror with serpents make

A hissing in this heart's mistake

Grave

10-22-21 22:48

My heart has bled itself dry

It beat too fast and flew too high

It gathered notions deep inside

That festered madly behind the lies

And still I wonder what's the use

To question all the fickle moods

Or shall I hang my head in shame

Knowing I am quite insane

To hang my heart upon a noose

And expect a ghost to cut me loose

As if I were a lovely soul

As if my life was good at all

And not the ugly things I hide

And how my heart has long since died

I fell to dream in fitful turns

10-25-21 14:53

I fell to dream in fitful turns

I lied awake beside an urn

It whispered of the secrets here

It tainted up the morning air

It plagued a mind with wanton flair

It laughed a tune in bitter fear

And lain upon the churning heart

Was stained the word, 'Forever part;"

For in this world we're all fools

Who wandered here amidst the mares

But never have we ever dared

To admit our dreams have faded

POETRY KRISTINE HOPE

Caught by a Dream

10-29-21 00:31, 00:46

I

  I covertly covet

You.

Caught catching dreams

In your catcher

Waking to

  Midnight wanderings

 Adventuring the dreamscape

Of figments I dare not name;

For I asked

 The Dream Catcher

Once

  What made me dream of you?

It simply replied

Not,

  But with soft sighings

 Instead of an inscription of

Fate

 It whispered in the wind

That lovers

Like us

  Often fight the fire

Only to get

Swept out, unprepared

In the eye

   Of a storm surging

We hadn't even noticed

Too busy with our insurgence

Against life's

  Fickle plot for the damned souls

Destined to doldrums;

 Indignant and whirling

We battled with a fury

Kept bottled for

 Decades

Only to come rushing

As slave against tyrant

  As the fool to the heart

    Like a Queen

And her knight

     Charging towards a new horizon

      Striving for that great unknown

Where Art My Marrow
10-29-21 12:57
I sucked out the marrow of life
I begged for it to enrapture me
In my suffocating mundanity
That threatens to overwhelm my
Sanity; oh, who am I

Now?

Lost without a notion of my past
Which had been lurking in dark corners
Where the shadows laugh,
A sour sickness overtaking my mind

And now?

I wish to break my skull upon the
Taut strings of my heart so that
My soul will finally learn that yearning
Is a curse I've yet to know

Yet, now...

I suffer the silence of stifling
Restrains that wormed their way
Inside my brain to taint what's left
Of a fading and failing mind

Still, here, I beseech thee—

Oh life, oh life, will I ever stop
Throwing my soul to sea
Expecting all the while to fly
Only to sink, burdened, beneath?

Trapped in a Wish

11-1-21 23:15

I am trapped

   And I am sinking

I've been blinking

   To blind my thinking

That my life is painted in violent patterns

That has been woven in my skin

It wavers still, like wishful woes

It creeps along, my awkward steps

And sings a tune, a soul bereft

To find a reason to live again

To shut the dark and hold a friend

Mesmerized by the vibrant hues

That dance upon distant views

To foretell a life that never could

Thrive inside the wishing wells

Where I fall, sinking still

My One & Only

11-24-21 23:10

 I need you in my life

To shelter heart from storm,

To gather all the clouds

And know they're not to mourn;

I need you by my side

To hold my frigid hand,

To give to me the warmth

My soul has long not had—

I need you next to me

So we may dance the beat

Of a life I'll live anew

Living, breathing, loving

Beside the one and only You

POETRY KRISTINE HOPE

Permeate

12-8-21 02:24

You've taught me more

Than I'd learn in a lifetime

You've shown me parts of my soul

I never knew

You've brought me to a world

I thought was only in movies

In your eyes, your smile, your laughter

I see heaven

In your heart, your mind, your aura

I see you

You mean more to me than I could

Ever articulate in words

You are the brightest star

And my gaze blazes at the sight—

I shall forever marvel at the

Moment I met You

Crazy We Crave
12-16-21 18:28
You did indeed shatter the dream
Only to leave me stranded at the train tracks
Betwixt ecstasy and oblivion— and the later

Tasted like dry wine in a pool of chaos;
And I thirsted for the flames of

Salvation

While you, unfazed, carried on
As if you hadn't trampled my heart in
Your haste to leave me in

Ruination

Yet I, even as I drifted in despair
Even as I walked the shores of

Emptiness

I still searched for Love; that salve
Which would dissolve the frost
In my aching soul and I

I found it. I found it in My Knight.

He rescued me from a land of
Frenzied confusion where the
Animals danced in hypnotic
Disarray in order to showcase a
Beauty hidden in the depths of
Their unbidden souls; the truth of
Gods

He swept me in his iron arms and
Told me the world should never
Be served, rather the world should
Bend to my will or why have a will at all
When it's trampled like dirt

He melted my heart against his own
And held me in the darkness that threatened;
Never should I fear again
The monsters in my life—
Never will I question then
The love between Him and I.

He shed a light inside my soul, a tune
Inside my heart~
We shall dance at the edge of oblivion,
And laugh, madly and wildly,
At the chaos that could not

Destroy the craziness we crave

For Once
12-28-21 13:30
Sometimes you need to see your soul
Reflected in others
In order to recognize your own fear
Holding you back
  From living life at all
  To finally let yourself feel, for once
All the chaos you try to minimize
  And recognize, after all

You matter, too.

                Even if it's hard to believe,
You deserve happiness;
          Despite your doubt—

Your fear can no longer be
            The reason to run from

    Embracing every creeping moment life brings at sunrise, until the day is eaten by the moon and the stars shine and you can finally sigh, with release

        Knowing that you are loved

And trying to love yourself, too; for after all,

  How could you not at least try to love the object of your own partner's affection?

  It is the truest test of life at this moment.
  It is the epitome of reinventing the foundation

 Of everything your mind said to believe;
  Only this time,
            You stop yourself before you fall.

This time, you know you matter, for once.

www.ingramcontent.com/pod-product-compliance
Lightning Source LLC
Chambersburg PA
CBHW020805160426
43192CB00006B/446